ULTRA DEEP FIELD

ULTRA DEEP FIELD

Poems by Ace Boggess

BRICK ROAD

POETRY PRESS

Library of Congress Control Number: 2017942834
ISBN-13: 978-0-9979559-2-7

Published by Brick Road Poetry Press
513 Broadway
Columbus, GA 31902-0751
www.brickroadpoetrypress.com

Brick Road logo by Dwight New

Other Books by Ace Boggess

Poetry
The Beautiful Girl Whose Wish Was Not Fulfilled
Wild Sweet Notes II: More Great Poetry from West Virginia (editor)
The Prisoners

Fiction
A Song Without a Melody

for my mother

Acknowledgments

The author wishes to thank the following publications in which these poems first appeared, sometimes in slightly different forms:

The Adirondack Review: "The Late Pablo Neruda"
Appalachian Heritage: "Power Outage"
The Aurorean: "The Good Poem"
Blue Monday Review: "Doodling on the Heavens"
The Bluestone Review: "Jar-O-Pain"
Bryant Literary Review: "Microwave Popcorn" and "The Dictionary"
Cider Press Review: "Ask Away"
Coe Review: "A Woman's Apartment" and "In Deference to the
        Thunderstorm"
Concho River Review: "Things I Want to See"
Connecticut River Review: "Noise" and "The Sci-Fi Lit Class"
Constellations: "It's Raining at 6 a.m."
The Cultural Weekly: "The English Language"
Devilfish Review: "Spider in the Clothes Pile"
East Coast Literary Review: "When the Guests Arrive"
Eunoia Review: "Horoscope," "Self-medication" and "Forgiveness"
Fourteen Hills: "The Test"
Fox Cry Review: "Letter to the Psychic Whose Ad I Found Inside a
        Used Book Twenty Years Later"
The Hamilton Stone Review: "A Light Dusting of Snow"
Heavy Feather Review: "Schoolteacher Elegy," "Butterfingers" and
        "The Postman"
Ikleftiko: "Letter to the Turkey Vulture on the Side of the Road
        Eating a Dead Deer's Eye"
Illya's Honey: "I'm Sorry Wilson Pickering"
Iodine Poetry Journal: "Infamy"
I-70 Review: "Rubbernecking"
Jenny: "Fake Orchids" and "Montana"
J Journal: "Home Confinement"
Kentucky Review: "Don't Forget"
Kestrel: "The New Journalism"
The Lake: "The Oops Observance"
Linden Avenue Literary Journal: "Irides"
Lost Coast Review: "I Take My New Girlfriend to the Gynecologist"

Masque & Spectacle: "Winter Morning" and "Unable to Sleep at 4 a.m."

Mid-American Review: "Potato Chip Sandwich"

Moon City Review: "Something Important"

Off the Coast: "Letter to a Friend I Dreamt Arrested as a Serial Killer"

The Old Red Kimono: "Bathroom Metaphysics"

The Orange Room Review: "The Fawn"

Poetry East: "Oh Nothing"

Poppy Road Review: "Letter to the Woman Who Waited Almost Twenty Years for Her Lover to Return"

The Provo Canyon Review: "What Was Lost"

RATTLE: "Mango Smoothie" and "Watching *The Wizard of Oz* in Prison"

red booth review: "Return Visit to Morgantown, West Virginia"

Rogue Agent: "My Other Life"

Sandy River Review: "Scientists Reportedly Discover Gate to Hell" and "Sexual"

Santa Fe Literary Review: "The Eye"

Saranac Review: "Russian Man Stabs Friend to Death for Preferring Prose to Poetry" and "The Frozen Breath"

SEEMS: "Breath" and "Repentance"

Southern Humanities Review: "The Times"

The Squalor Review: "The Model"

Sugar House Review: "Letter to the Funeral Director Who Fell Down While Pulling a Gurney Up a Flight of Stairs" and "Elegy for the Audience"

Tar River Poetry: "Nor'easter"

Tendril: "After Words"

The Tishman Review: "Groom"

West Trade Review: "Things You Don't Know You'll Miss"

Whale Road Review: "A Religious Discussion"

Wilderness House Literary Review: "Ultra Deep Field"

Yellow Chair Review: "Identity Theory"

Zaira Journal: "Meeting My Lover for Lunch"

Contents

I. Being & Nothingness

Ask Away *5*

Potato Chip Sandwich *6*

The Late Pablo Neruda *7*

Elegy for the Audience *8*

Letter to the Funeral Director Who Fell Down While Pulling a Gurney Up a Flight

        of Stairs *9*

Noise *10*

Schoolteacher Elegy *11*

Butterfingers *12*

Ultra Deep Field *13*

Horoscope *14*

Infamy *15*

Forgiveness *16*

Trash Day *17*

The Frozen Breath *18*

Russian Man Stabs Friend to Death for Preferring Prose to Poetry *20*

A Religious Discussion *21*

Bathroom Metaphysics *22*

Things I Want to See *23*

Montana *24*

Jar-O-Pain *25*

II. Being & Time

The Times *29*

The New Journalism *30*

The Sci-fi Lit Class *31*

Spider in the Clothes Pile *32*

My Other Life *33*

When the Guests Arrive *34*

The Postman *35*

What Was Lost *36*

A Light Dusting of Snow *37*

Winter Morning *38*

Unable to Sleep at 4 a.m. *39*

Letter to the Woman Who Waited Almost Twenty Years for Her Lover to Return *40*

Microwave Popcorn *41*

Watching The Wizard of Oz in Prison *43*

It's Raining at 6 a.m. *44*

Sexual *45*

The Model *46*

Letter to a Friend I Dreamt Arrested as a Serial Killer *47*

Doodling on the Heavens *48*

Fake Orchids *49*

Letter to the Psychic Whose Ad I Found Inside a Used Book Twenty Years Later *50*

Things You Don't Know You'll Miss *51*

Don't Forget *53*

III. Being There

Mango Smoothie *57*

Irides *58*

Nor'easter *59*

The Good Poem *61*

I Take My New Girlfriend to the Gynecologist *62*

I'm Sorry Wilson Pickering *63*

The Oops Observance *64*

Identity Theory *65*

"Scientists Reportedly Discover Gate to Hell" *66*

The Fawn *67*

Letter to the Turkey Vulture on the Side of the Road Eating a Dead Deer's Eye *68*

Oh Nothing *69*

Meeting My Lover for Lunch *70*

Breath...71

Repentance..72

Something Important...73

The English Language...74

The Eye..75

Rubbernecking...76

Letter to the Guy in the White Sedan Yelling "Hey Asshole!" at the Driver of the
    Burgundy Van in Front..77

A Woman's Apartment..78

Home Confinement...79

The Dictionary...81

The Express...82

In Deference to the Thunderstorm..83

Groom..85

Return Visit to Morgantown, West Virginia...86

Letter to a Wound..87

Self-medication..88

Letter to Four Old Postmen Every Day at Noon Playing Dominoes at a Table
    in the Gino's Pizza and Spaghetti House...................................89

The Test...90

After Words..91

Power Outage...92

Letter to a Droplet of Water..93

Gamble...94

"Thanks for Ending Your Poems"...95

About the Author...96

Breath...71

Repentance..72

Something Important...73

The English Language...74

The Eye...75

Rubbernecking...76

Letter to the Guy in the White Sedan Yelling "Hey Asshole!" at the Driver of the

    Burgundy Van in Front..77

A Woman's Apartment 78

Home Confinement 79

The Dictionary..81

The Express 82

In Deference to the Thunderstorm 83

Groom 85

Return Visit to Morgantown, West Virginia...86

Letter to a Wound...87

Self-medication 88

Letter to Four Old Postmen Every Day at Noon Playing Dominoes at a Table

    in the Gino's Pizza and Spaghetti House 89

The Test 90

After Words 91

Power Outage..92

Letter to a Droplet of Water 93

Gamble...94

"Thanks for Ending Your Poems" 95

About the Author...96

Ask Away

ask me about the radiant hat
moon makes for that cloud face an hour before dawn

ask me about sitting on gravel staring through a
            playground fence
waiting like a godless monk for my mother to arrive

ask me how my hands trembled squeezing the knife
that cut me & drew new lines on stranger skin than mine

ask me about fidelity whether high or in-
how bodies in darkness cling to forgotten music

ask me why she put the cat out before she closed the door
ask me why I stayed ask me ask

ask also about softness &
how easy it is to name those better times

ask me why beautiful moments rob entire days of their
            despair
or why truth may be painful but it's never personal

ask me what I did to deserve this &
what I did not do when the corner choir sang its shadows

ask me if & when & who the great who-done-it
it was I in the study with a candlestick

ask me nothing & I will wish no honest words
like forgiveness to be muttered in the dark

Potato Chip Sandwich

the beauty of poverty
is its compulsion to invention

lighting cigarettes off the stove
extending the life of toilet tissue

the potato chip sandwich
Lord the potato chip sandwich

riffled valleys crunching on a bun
unity of firm & soft

salty & muted as a chaste kiss
twigs snapping once twice

casting off hunger
like Neruda's sad nets

into that fulfilling sea
of his lover's eyes

The Late Pablo Neruda

they dig him up because his silence
booms as loudly as the shells of Pinochet

they dig him up because if there were a murderer
he might have been close he might have heard

a final verse whispered to the drawing sheet
a last gasp a prayer a sonnet filled with desolation

they dig in hope he will write the denouement
to soften tension from his falling action

even in desiccated fingers dents of pens
wait to fill again the world with language

through old soil the diggers as they hope exhume
a last song for Matilde & the sea that moved him

or a psalm of protest denouncing those who fail
to note distinctions between tanks & temple bells

Elegy for the Audience

no matter what the minister says he does not know
if this man made arrangements with the Christian god

Jewish god or the no-god-at-all
in an emptiness of interconnected atoms

fire raged & fire dimmed to whispered snaps of twigs
in between a man danced with feet of a surgeon

the rhythm of an umber leaf
testing wind from the ground

as you dance now
silent & afraid to cry out in too-piercing voice

that life is a song on the radio
fractured with static & playing on

while you slide with heavy steps
into another room

Letter to the Funeral Director
Who Fell Down While Pulling
a Gurney Up a Flight of Stairs

with what ease life makes its presence known
in that hour its twin raises the jeweled scepter

like a sacred clown before your Native tribe
you perform this sudden slapstick

a comedy of errors to teach us
there waits movement underneath the flesh

what it means to be human
even when we wear the granite face of loss

you fall & are falling forever
like a baseball tossed from orbit

at least you have others to bear the deceased
while your legs stiffen straighten stretch

as solemn as the skull of Yorick in its grave
when the spotlight dims the ritual remains

Noise

sit by the phone that never rings
awaiting whatever silence follows silence

a black cat shrieks unheard from the street
while a lime-green truck shreds linings of its brakes

there's disparaging thunder in some other distant place
wind cursing gods & rooftops of the world

new lovers bellow in delightful agony
while regret deep-throats its mantras for tomorrow &

still the phone that doesn't ring doesn't ring
still the stillness of losing oh that lost art of the lost

Schoolteacher Elegy

scanning the obituaries this morning I see
my junior high English teacher

the one who ignored me while I slept or pretended to sleep
with head posed on arm pressed to the desk

then introduced me to Hugo the French Shakespeare
with Quasimodo's bones cradling a rose in Esmeralda's grave

I was a child in hiding then
afraid even to speak my name aloud

yet she had me doing voices as I read my part
from a play filled with spacemen & the humor of the human

life is a literary tragedy from birth & also a comedy of errors
as though a sign waits inside each coffin urging *Watch for falling rocks*

I would return the favor & let her sleep
or pretend as though dead actors must come back with bows

but first a grateful nod for the calamity of words
crashing together on a page

buried these many years in the last place
I ever thought to look

Butterfingers

the whir of its rolling like a bowling ball in the return
then silence before it clicks the pavement

it hops like a child's red bouncer from a coin machine
stops inches from encountering my shoe

forbidden fruit in the Eden of sprites
fleshy marble dropped from a height

yet no crabapple roots near the perimeter of the house
this jewel smuggled a long way to the roof

by a clumsy squirrel losing his grip at last
before the meat might make a meal for his chattering mouth

snatching defeat from the jaws of victory as a professor of mine
once said turning the clichéd into a newsworthy line

also he was adamant we feel bad not badly *never* badly
for someone & bad is what I feel for this journeyman down on his
      luck

who left his luggage on a southbound train
I was like him earlier when my fingers slipped their grip on a coffee
      mug

I watched it fall endlessly as though in Xeno's paradox
heading forever by halves to the floor

Ultra Deep Field

"Whenever we don't understand something, we call it dark."
—Father Corbally of the Vatican Observatory

to free eyes from the keyholes of the skull
give them feet for walking crystal ladders

how better to seek out the Infinite
than exploring farthest bubble edges of the finite?

what appear to be stars are galaxies so distant
no one thought to look

so much to measure in these shaded fascinations
wherever the Artist scattered paint

polishing a long lens more delicate than skin
the Franciscan nods as he announces "I don't know"

the human answer not the holiest: "don't know"
he says to questions about life destruction some space-

booted intergalactic one true God "I don't know"
his light heart full with unseen matter

Horoscope

you will die a horrible death
you will die stained by newsprint in a gutter

unloved you limp club-
footed to your grave

as if made of bronze your shoulder blades
perfect a coming feast for pigeons

your eyes my god your eyes
gaze boldly at the bull that blinds them

you are destined to linger cheerless &
smitten with one deceased before you

your sons will die before you
your songs will die before you

the Dean *de los muertos* expels you
from the course on candied skulls

your final breath must be as bitter as
old coffee oils & vinegar that cleanses them

a last lipstick rose shall wilt
weeping in the lonely chamber of your wake

Infamy

they will say of me
I carved my poems with a kitchen knife

my iambs became I-wants
my rhythm staccato as a broken faucet

they will say I should spend my life
writing in the language of remorse

Forgiveness

the underworld gives back its dead
the flood gives back its rivulets of rain

back unseen go gamma rays
through distant zones of darkly-mattered space

goodbye hate-filled diatribes spit
by small men with bigger ideas about themselves

plastic jugs escape their fate fifty feet deep in the burning dump
to be refilled by milk that sweetest sap

the universe contracts
the Earth runs backward in its weeping eye

heat cools & ice bursts into steam
songs of lost singers echo again from the lips of this new life

I rescind the words I never said aloud
those that sting my lungs like fangs of smoke

as a dandelion blesses the mower's blade
gluing the seedhead to its slender neck

Trash Day

black bags swollen with debris
knotted to keep the worst from spilling out

in less than an hour the city crew
will back its beeping hearse up to the curb &

carry off fried chicken & fruit trays
a half-eaten cake

dozens of Styrofoam cups
like silent candles cool & dim

paper plates stitched together
with casseroles

all those things we throw away
to avoid recalling clutter that remains

that vinegary stench can be unbearable
old meat & berries saved too long

their stink a hodgepodge
of our unrewarded miseries

it's difficult enough
without the arrogance & waste

or the sound of my mother
crying in another room

The Frozen Breath

in weeks
after the Towers fell

I often read how attendance
at religious services went up

as with promiscuous sex
drug & alcohol abuse

& aggregate sales
of ice cream

God is always good for a catastrophe
one understands the impulse

to orgasm & oblivion
but how do people convert

a metropolitan nightmare
into Neapolitan delight?

why are there no country songs
about drowning sorrows

in a Creamsicle shake?
maybe we needed the frozen breath

the icy inhale off a chocolate sundae
to quench fires

we still saw raging from that day
the demon face of smoke & flame

newspapers flaunted
as the internet scripted it into legend

maybe we wanted to feel the innocence
of childhood

when what we knew of war
was a ballgame

followed by a slice of pizza
dripping off its plate

maybe God's phone lines were busy
while our bodies

rejected their secret pleasures
& escapes

maybe we just hoped to forget
life was ever anything but sweet

Russian Man Stabs Friend to Death
for Preferring Prose to Poetry

—wire reports, January 29, 2014

I'd name you Raskolnikov but that would be the other gent
if his feet wore bloody socks so ripe with rage & arrogance

you put down the brothers K & sided with the Brodskyites
leveling a cherry orchard with your flowery knife

in fevered voice he spoke for Turgenev & Solzhenitsyn
but your response was hardly the soft murmur of a
        Christian

however Orthodox your vision of this world might be
it lacks the horrors brush-stroked in your crimson artistry

how you carved the iambs from his Russian heart
dense his prose & guttural like a bear at karaoke mimicking
        a lark

did your hero Koltsov in his wisdom tell you *Be a blade
again*? or did you *drink life's cup with thirsty lips* vis-à-vis
        Mikhail

Lermontov? such a shame I doubt those stately men of
        verse
would send your comrade on his way in the shady winter of
        a hearse

A Religious Discussion

the chaplain asked if I believe in anything
he seemed kind with his silver hair

round flushed face & history too like mine
his travels through addiction his time behind bars

so I didn't give the usual *not-your-business*
I said my god speaks to me in my language

which means he often says "go fuck yourself"
or "look at the balls on this guy" I mean

why would I trust anyone who won't point out
when I'm being an asshole or need to get to work?

no use these days for parables of goats
for bread alone—have you seen the prison food?

the chaplain asked "but what happens
when you wake up panicked after midnight &

need comforted?" I said he tells me
"go back to sleep you shitheel when you wake up

it's one day closer to the end of the world
one day closer to home"

Bathroom Metaphysics

the sink overflows with righteousness
sinners speckled like bird eggs drown in the swirling font

the mirror is the lie God tells Himself just before taking stage
to sin or juggle the platypus & Chinese population

the toilet proclaims itself sink without conscience
roaring Hallelujahs absolving anyone with pennies

the tissue paper knows no mythology its atheists in the foxhole
ruggedly fighting to secure the southern front

the wall is illusion man can be One with the world beyond
a hungry hitchhiking Buddha standing in the road to block his way

Things I Want to See

traveling back roads of old America
I should pause to witness largest balls of twine & foil

to seek out haunted granaries
or battlefields where blackish soil runs red at night

& yet unmoved I feel as if I drank the lotus wine
unable to journey home from the museum of shoes

why does a man wait for adventure
until all crumbs are eaten from the trail?

somewhere the candy boss gives guided tours
somewhere a portal opens

into mystery magnificence or curiosity
I want to see the greatest hiccoughs of the Earth

the collections of dust & antiquated toys
if only my feet could jump this fence

or dance a sidestep past the guards
who watch from every angle of my neck

Montana

all prisoners dream of escaping to Montana
where the long arm of the law bends back to scratch an itch

my brother's wife left him for Montana
it's peaceful there & wedding vows

dissolve like the poetry of whippoorwills
at night beneath intense almost reachable skies

the carnies never pull shenanigans in Montana
bottles fall & teddy bears reach the size of Labradors

"papa when I die will I go to Montana?"
has been heard a bit too often in these parts

the quickest way to Montana is a fast ship
the quickest way to Montana is to be caught cheating at poker

Montana's nearest hospital waits in North Dakota
the morgue Wyoming the graveyard deep in Texas

O Lord please show me the wonders of Montana
its diamond mines & shimmering cities of gold

though I walk through the valley of the shadow of Montana
I fear nothing for Thou art with me

Jar-O-Pain

the mechanic's waiting room its metallic screams
a man with one eye says "have you been here long?"

I find a gallery of curiosities who could expect
a popcorn maker with colossal iron wheels

relic from some one-screen movie house
or the antique *RC Cola* dispenser many decades old?

pennants from the Pittsburgh Steelers' teams of the 1970s
exalt past glories like old men seated on the barber's steps

while photos spotlight victories by a boxer
whose name is as forgotten as his hair's bulbous cut

I almost smell that musky stink of sweat
from his arms broad like boulders leaning on a ledge

even sounds of torture from the bay beyond a far wall
are muted beneath crackling Satchmo radio notes

yet on the counter a clear glass urn recalls the horrible
purpose of the place: *Jar-O-Pain* its label—

a curio cabinet for screws tacks rust-covered nails
bottle shards & half a scissor blade

"pulled those out of tires" says a man at the register
he smiles beneath his mustache

I nod then spend an hour staring at the jar
its masters have filled it with my imagination:

a Mayan dagger used to carve a heart
steel fingers from Torquemada's bag of tricks

shark's tooth & a serpent with jaw unhinged
a chainsaw-wielding psycho in a mask

when the mechanic enters & says "all done"
I'm unable to think of anything now but hurt

II. Being & Time

II. Being & Time

The Times

earbuds plugged into their aural sheaths
I'm listening again to classic Dylan

his indiscreet protests his cries of contempt
for bloodshed & also indifference

his day's culture clung to like a rock deep in the flood
until he came along until he enchanted them with outrage

left them amped & pissed & fighting back
I try to understand this to take it in

as I'm bobbing bird-like to the strum &
there he goes once more soloing on his harmonica

each tone trilled hits my broken molar's nerve
like ice cream or an errant dentist's drill

I wince grunt hold my breath
bite my lip to suffer back the ache

hoping the guns along the front will silence
hoping the bone saw will cease to carve the dead

this is how you relate to *the horror the horror*
the angst & misery of that distant time

you close your eyes & grit your teeth &
come to it not with empathy but with pain

The New Journalism

staff a newspaper with artists & dreamers &
I would be the editor-in-chief "go

to the battlefield" I would say "where
bodies lie drawn to points like croquet balls

look up then left find the sunset approach &
tell its story" above the fold page one

for the *Local* section "ask a murderer about his child-
hood sweetheart" & "get photographs" this the news I love

I don't want to know why the chicken crossed the road
but why he is a chicken when he could've been a fish

blood splashes everywhere across the daily pages
so I reject the who what when where & why

I'd frame the image then hang it in a gallery
where thoughtful patrons measure its angles

the texture density painter's intent
let them decide where beauty meets brutality

in the alleyways of rain-sick dark
under covers where lovers & children hide

"jumper on the 6th Street Bridge" I'd say
"get over there and take someone from *Sports*"

The Sci-fi Lit Class

how seriously Prof. Gerke took the subject
outlining & diagramming his mathematical formulas

he said it's about extrapolation from dust specks to deserts
I came in thinking lasers & bug-

eyed beasts with sharp teeth
but he advised prophecy too from pragmatic roots

predicting solar cars & geodesic domes
colleagues chatting face to face on their tiny phones

while I wanted to escape the wars & religions of the world
he said think about it *think think*—*grok* a better word—

how guns will silence themselves
only when better guns appear &

gods wear different masks
to reveal their old ideas to a new public

look ahead but first look back: we have been here
we have been this way before

Spider in the Clothes Pile

never have I seen one so large indoors
a baby's fist with bristles visible on its back

black as the fusion crust on a meteorite
black as any imagined spider black

the Platonic universal waiting in its cave
of boxers & coffee-stained tees

I go to pick them up & out it drops: the black spot
of old Blind Pew on my biblical beige carpet

God how I must have sounded: part shriek
part the ach-ach-ach of a hairball-spewing cat

double fright: the it that is & it the unexpected
a spider in the clothes pile heart-shocks

spikes the pulse though to say it out loud
makes me think of "A Buddha in the Woodpile"

the poem by Ferlinghetti about Waco
the cult whackos & whackos in the FBI

all that violence when a Buddha would bring peace
but if a Buddha fell out of my clothes pile

I'd have been just as frightened
maybe more despite his *Om*ing & *Ah*ing

or sweet gentleness of his enlightened eyes
because for fuck's sake how did he get in there? &

as he crawled toward safety of the under-bed
his head would be too big for my well-aimed shoe

My Other Life

taught me I can
take a beating

a fist burning
with my blood

raised in the night
like a banner

I know what it's like
to fall

as in *The Fall*
religious

deficiency
no pills for that

I learned too
how to hide

which I knew already
even in a crowd

the trick is
to say nothing

like the corpse
in a stage play

we've trained our-
selves if someone

doesn't speak
he isn't there

When the Guests Arrive

too many strangers the old man sees
luminescent phantoms that stalk his avenues of mind

there's Charlie behind you drowning help him please &
John who sits starving in a corner of the room

next comes a man—six-four & night black—he doesn't like
the one who tries to grab his second penis

which if women are right & the first is the seat for a man's brain
would be the home of telepathy & second sight

in the old man's case a lonely vision
his eyes inverse kaleidoscopes of fractured dark

he spies on this other-verse
inviting new guests to the party every night

as if the bed he never leaves cannot contain him &
he will dance a sideways step nearing the door

The Postman

all my life I've been waiting for the postman
with his answers to so many questions

spoken in the gruff or desperate voices of strangers
each the next exit on an Interstate highway of words

hold up I've often wished to say
let's have some coffee & a crust of cinnamon toast

he passes in & out of my life
like the silence after rain before crickets tune their clarinets

give me a thought on politics or epistemology
I'd beg although he leaves me bank statements

electric bills & ads for services I never use
then it's back to the wait & next delay

like a curved eye left half-carved in stone
unable to see while incomplete what it wouldn't see if whole

What Was Lost

fishing the Poca River once my stepbrother
caught his line on the motor of a passing boat

I watched the aged & beaten rod shoot off
like squirting catsup from a squeeze bottle

slip his grip then disappear beneath the muddy plane
we were too young then to believe in absurdities

like what would be his best fish story
about the time he caught a boat though he never tells it

preferring his other tale of loss
how robbers cleaned him out

then took the urn holding his father's ashes
another vanishing act another piece

of life swallowed up by the invisible
the not-knowing like in Schrödinger's hypothetical

if some sneak thief released the cat & stole the box
leaving nothing but uncertainty & a lot of rage:

the only possessions a man can have
that no one ever wants to take away

A Light Dusting of Snow

is not enough to make my mother curse
the ground the sky the hazards of the road

to prevent her going where she goes
when work enforces its rite

to conjure her from the thinly shadowed
wasteland of a Saturday

how that sheer cotton raiment
bares grasses exposes fingers

from young spring flowers reaching
for the door too soon

this will not prevent her leaving
for exercise or groceries

it is not enough to coerce her
into weeping at perfection

she has witnessed many snows
never have I seen her weep for one

Winter Morning

leaves rustle in chill wind
deep-

throated winter birds
that sing in whispers

snow on the ground
not everywhere

hints
like a woman in a partly revealing dress

the road empty of all but ghosts
of travelers

Unable to Sleep at 4 a.m.

the first dream in weeks pays its extorted toll &
in it I am the horror

assassin sci-fi samurai slaughtering
the alien in the alien

landscape of this videogame
blood like a parasite slithers through my chest

I must not snack before bedtime
I must not read Camus

the darkness before darkness comes
sings like burning timber in my head

sleep murders itself this night
I slip on shoes & jacket

go outside to smoke
go inside to make coffee

nighttime mocks cajoles scatters salt everywhere
as if to test the old wound

yet even without rest there is no restlessness
I cannot sleep but enjoy it more than I endure it

I even pause to watch
the snow pasted to a table out front

it does nothing never moves
my forehead touches window glass

my breathing slows
I have learned how to rest with my eyes

Letter to the Woman Who Waited Almost Twenty Years for Her Lover to Return

Garcia-Marquez would embrace you with his pen
not woman at all but the illusion of one

walking motley avenues in fairy-tale
kingdoms of obsession & the heart

you are not real—that is I never say
you are not real but I make you as I go

out of granite splashed with drops of lavender oil
a form revealed from rather than carved in stone

how does one starve so long in a kitchen
stocked with soups plus bread & candied yams?

yet all those working hours have cashed their checks
gone home to sleep forever next to their forgetful wives

why did you wait like a moon beyond its tides
while Odysseus slept in the arms of many seas?

Microwave Popcorn

in the movie theaters of my childhood
I learned to love the dark

before the first flicker
before the spaceship cowboy man with a golden gun

smirked cynically into existence
as even family dissipated into unreality

it was only me & the void &
the bucket of popcorn buttery & lukewarm

oily fingers touching salted lips
teeth crunching tree limbs & brittle bones

I made myself boy king in the land of shadows
collecting my tribute by handfuls

now I place my booty in a little metal box
punch a few numbers then listen

for the hum & for loudspeakers
from the beta-test room at the fireworks factory

the freedom darkness brings &
the anticipation are gone

cinematic majesty & magic
disbanded in favor of the parceling of pixels

only the corn remains
an artifact from a bygone culture

homogenized standardized bastardized
the way vitamin tablets replace the haloed orange

I'm glad you are dead Orville Redenbacher
you have stolen my youth &

here in this emasculated imagination of middle age
I curse each grain I swallow

then beg forgiveness
for the terrible damnation taken in

Watching *The Wizard of Oz* in Prison

we sit there straining & stiff
in straight-backed chairs

half a dozen of us
following Dorothy's naïve plunge

into trouble & Technicolor
a fantasy less enchanting

than in the innocence of our youth
what is Dot but a body dressed in innocence?

her Betty Boop *oh-my*s
her dance-stepping along the avenues

like a skipped stone or drop of paint
from a bucket left on a booming speaker &

how she makes friends with strangers
what her mama warned her about

more likely to encounter one of us
cowardly heartless & out of our minds

we forgive her this slip-up
having come with her so far

we go on following at a safe distance
like guardian angels with bloody swords &

when we arrive at the Emerald City
we sneak thief-like through the gates

wanting to see her achieve her goal
which is the same as ours

It's Raining at 6 a.m.

it's coming down while I am coming up
it sings to me *Rest* in a choir of violence

sun too has dreamt itself away
to a world in which it has no need for rising

outside a window long grass buckles
beneath the lashes from so many heavy blows

I need another word for *green* that holds more *gray*
a word without the connotation *inexperienced*

no virgins coyly hide their faces in the storm
cleansing merges with decay

like a second-hand store filled with impurities
where even scents of leather mixed with dog hair fade

now I force myself from bed but still I'm sleeping
when the roof applauds all men take their bows

Sexual

the bifurcated smoke bands up & bends
a helix of human bodies in motion

they lack hands but naked backs
ripple & writhe in their rising passion

a man & woman two women or men
their skins transform too rapidly for a dull lens

to summarize their pornography
silver-blue erotica a hologram

afloat like pigeon feathers on the wind
how they embrace turn wrestle for control

there a slender thigh buttock shoulder blade
there for an instant eyes

The Model

lines body lines soft blurring curving turning pitch
on a tuning fork golden straights & narrows

lines making a bat's ears from the armpits
thighs loose cannons that sink a sturdy ship

lines traced with fingertips the pillar of throat
the eye of the mouth the thousand curlicues

like blackened limbs the true art is painting
shadows & the lines that run to infinity

Letter to a Friend I Dreamt
Arrested as a Serial Killer

no time to apologize
neither you to the dead nor I the slandered

when asked *do you know him?* I knew
so meek a man simple starlight blinds

I have seen you shackled leg & wrist
bent-back in the burning orange of no remorse

silver beard pressed to chest how a spaniel's head bows
as if in prayer after whip-crack of *The Daily Mail*

I watched you on an old TV squared off
like a window through which I must doubt

the tulips & deny the oaks for their unreality
though at least I never saw the shallow graves

Doodling on the Heavens

because he has not had time to mourn her absence
because he has had nothing but time to mourn her absence

he has spent years thinking of her &
never thought of her

shoulders ice rinks for his skating fingers
eyes mood rings changing color with her tears & laughter

sad laughter laughable tears
the bottle held to her lips

as though she meant to speak her message into it
these are ideas clay & shadows

he never molds from them a vase
to hold her jagged lines

sometimes he tries to spell her name
from the alphabet soup of midnight's sky

but cannot find letters to match the images he draws
images that do not resemble her at all

images that resemble nothing
forsaken child doodling on the heavens

he plays with so much of this cosmic dust &
forgets dust is what made her

forgets dust can be scattered or wiped away &
returns first to the corners of the room

Fake Orchids

driver of the silver *Escalade* accelerates
to keep me longer from the turning lane

"can't believe he did that" says the woman beside me
"it's okay" I tell her "he needs fake orchids too &

knows he has to beat you to the home-goods store
before you buy them all" she smiles

shakes her head & with forgiveness
she ignites like a bag of flares

I want my Ph.D. in making women smile
I want the evidence against me

suppressed so I am innocent again
if I can erase gray of the highway

the gray of rain & sparkling haze of the *Escalade*
those many years spent muddling among blur lines

of my own adventure "fine" she says
as she cups my hand above the transaxle

"let's beat him" I say & at least today
I'm the protagonist of this film

with his favorite hat pistol notebooks &
one great line I haven't thought of yet

Letter to the Psychic Whose Ad I Found
Inside a Used Book Twenty Years Later

did you know I would turn a page & find you there
promising the future of the past? sleepless

I wandered dark avenues of possibility
how you might have pointed out the pitfalls

spared me scars & the old clichés: lost love & *if only*
for ten dollars my lifeline might have curved from dread

toward repose were you chaperone of my emerging now
I was a college boy learning to hold my liquor then & you

waited for a hand to hold with fierce tenderness
a priestess reciting drug-induced gospels to the lost

I missed you like a road sign for *Beware*
as I missed so much in my youth before it was too late

before I passed my exit & found my own wrong answers
like a kitten testing outlets with its claws

Things You Don't Know You'll Miss

dinner napkins fine linen coarse heavy cloth blood-
moon red the kind you drop on the floor pick up & wash

a butter knife or something with more edge
the blade not just the tender flesh it terrorizes

a fork its prongs divining rods for meat
the phone number for your favorite pizza place

or taxi service to anywhere
all things you hold leave holes in absence

black cat mobile phone coffee mug shaped like a skull
more than diplomas on the wall you rarely notice

like the love of your life who lingers in shadow
somewhere on the opposite side of a living room

there's the feel of your keys in a pocket
pressed like needful hands against your thigh

comforting reminding you can leave & return
the safety of the escape plan

the one you never use although you're glad to have it
like favorite films on DVDs you buy so you need not watch

does it make you uncomfortable to consider so much?
if there seems to be something missing there is

your cherished silk boxers your most hated pair of socks
that paisley tie that ends in disarray

a jar full of pennies how you despised pennies
now each heads-up harbors ghosts of more than Lincoln

could you imagine you might mourn for burnt-
out bulbs? a toilet brush? your grandfather's *Bible*

buried in a box in the garage? see how easy it is
to overlook so much when you feel you have so little

with even dust that stains the shoulders of your coat
carried off by a last gust from some unwelcome wind

Don't Forget

don't forget the watermelon
you asked me to remind you &

though my conscious
memory has been filled in

by sandstorms & Morse code
I thought I should leave you this note

with its brief demands
for your time

how bright the sun
shines this afternoon

how warm the air &
scented like an oven baking bread

but don't forget the watermelon
pink in the meat like lipstick

sweet with juice
fastening your fingers to your lips

III. Being There

Mango Smoothie

I come to your door with a mango smoothie
because you are sick your world inverse

like that *Star Trek* episode
where bad Spock's goatee reflects the Jolly Roger

leaning in I watch you sip sunny nectar
exhale only shadow

I know I cannot heal you
love never a healing word

as I know from your trailing mascara
you lack faith to keep this down for long

at least I have offered a favorable flavor
for the coming up again

like a bottle of sauce
to dress the lesser meat

Irides

how often I conjure them in the empty air
two olives in a clear martini glass

how they twitch staring into me
from nothing & nowhere

unripe crabapples dangling
on a rain-jade afternoon

all this imagining
all this redrafting

so I can know I possess a part of you
a photograph on memory paper

lidless &
milkless

computer animations of hurricanes
moving left across the screen

how I reach for them &
how they slip my grasp

those destroyers
of so many worlds of mine

Nor'easter

"don't have a heart attack"
the neighbor shouts as she stands by her box

her ancient eyes conspicuous with ancient sadness
the kind that comes from smallest disappointments

applied by doubt "do you think" she says
"the mail will run?" what does she expect?

a letter from her son? a government check?
some love note overdue by fifty years

lost behind the postman's rusty desk?
I wave my reassurance about all things

then return to shoveling—nine inches of pristine pack
a Styrofoam carton embracing the roads sidewalks stairs—

I want to say my back aches & my shoulders
but time enough for misery when no work remains

after I've exhumed stone bodies
from this great mass grave

another neighbor trudges down the lane
his boots crunching snow like autumn leaves

he brings two stacks of mail—envelopes
for the old woman & a book for me—

from the carrier whose Jeep
took a cowardly turn back down the hill

I thank him & we stand in silence
staring nodding needing nothing more

we share an infinite serenity
an instant of wellness in this unwell world

The Good Poem

I can say it now
my life made better for my having read

it tasted of cheeseburgers &
smelled like autumn just before the chill

it *was* a good poem
although I will forget it soon enough

the author's name already a burst of light that's flickered from the
        eye
I should go again though not today too soon too soon

the images still pulsing with the heartbeat of first reading
I gained hope & gave back an emotional response

my fingers twitched
I gulped hard as I swallowed doubt & yearning

yes a good poem a masterpiece
an eclipse seen in a pinhole box

I don't know what it meant but felt it kick me in a tender spot
then rub my shoulders & gently kiss my neck

it was a one-night stand I long to have again
a good poem a memory a shadow

I Take My New Girlfriend to the Gynecologist

this must be more than a fling
pause between lovers to catch my breath

what stillness comes from sharing her discomfort
at least sharing from safety of the parking lot

a journalist beyond the fence at Area 51
unwelcome to the mysteries there

for an hour I watch in my rearview
as women walk in & out & by

mostly young attractive shuffling feet
heads bowed as if ashamed to face the sky

signs on the wounded fence next door
advise No Trespassing & Beware of Dog

one might misread Beware of Doctor
see here comes a nurse radiant in ugly afterglow

smoking a long gray cigarette &
telling stories to someone on her phone

over there stands another man like me
waiting for bells to chime & a sermon to end

perhaps with a splash of water
perhaps an invocation

or a sin-eater stealing the horrors
whispering "go in peace" & "see you soon"

I'm Sorry Wilson Pickering

I look down & see I'm standing on your grave
its small bronze plate sans stone or earth-rise

I meant no disrespect but blinked & you were there
a flickering apparition of you haunting no one but yourself

besides who do you think you are anyway
to have died in 1890 four score plus one before my being
        born?

you're not here to tell me about some minor battle in the
        Civil War
in which you shot & killed a man for something you
        believed in once

leaving history to name you saint or cutlass-wielding pirate
except that history has forgotten you

not even a gadfly squashed between pages of a history text
who are you Wilson Pickering? your name

sounds an awful lot like Wilson Pickett
who sang "I've Come a Long Way" & "In the Midnight
        Hour"

doesn't matter you didn't stick around long enough
for rhythm & blues or even the beginning of the jazz age

oh but excuse me I must get back to the circle
Wilson Pickering I just wanted to let you know

I apologize for showing you the flats of my feet
to acknowledge you & maybe mourn a little

which is better than what I came for &
at best a moment's distraction for us both

The Oops Observance

enchantments rise on glossy porcelain pedestals for an hour
a man walks under a ladder & bad luck earns its annual flash

I'm sitting here on National Ballpoint Pen Day
my ballpoint pen in drag across the highways of a page

thinking *Why not have an American Oops Month?*
it would cover spilled soda on a new white carpet

car wrecks at 2 a.m. & brief but passionate love affairs
not to mention bombing the Chinese Embassy by accident

or invading the wrong small sovereign Arab nation
yes Reader you & I could revel in our festival of flaws

come raise a glass to that Oops observance
with its varied sighs & grand cache of calamities

its public farts & Y2K glitches in the existential code
we will boogie in our best funereal suits

Identity Theory

"Many people have to change a great deal and wear all sorts of clothes."
—Hermann Hesse, *Siddhartha*

I am still the young cub reporter who wore
his crooked tie like a noose cut just in time &

that kid black-teed in the record-shop back room
selling paraphernalia to what weirdoes wandered in

I'm naked dangling dumbly in bed or
the delousing bath at the gateway to some prison

which is real? tweed jacket?
burnt orange jailhouse jumper?

my freshman poly-sci prof said "good argument
if it didn't come from a guy in a *KISS* tee shirt"

there have been sweaters too so many sweaters
plain bland ugly green & gray

I am a man who wears sweaters
I'm a man who wears the past like a sack of bones

"Scientists Reportedly Discover Gate to Hell"

—*Yahoo News*, April 2, 2013

look close to see contrails of music burn
on stairs where Orpheus dropped his wordless voice

stairs Dante descended in a dream
in search of the better solution to loss

now come scholars sick with finding
knowing dread the first time in millennia

oh vapor oh blessed curse oh Pluto's Gate
that pyre oh that carrion breath

slaughters every bird fed to its mouth
before so much as a rush to reach the teeth

yet nowhere a sign demands *Abandon Hope*
those crossing already hope-burst

proving the seeking scientists are fools
to the greater glory of us all

The Fawn

bounds up the yard
its salted body wobbling

like a frigate storm-
tossed across the undulating sea

it knows no violence
but absence

separated from its mother
by an unmeshed fence &

all the uncertainty
that freedom is

Letter to the Turkey Vulture on the Side
of the Road Eating a Dead Deer's Eye

you have to be the ugliest ferryman
for souls of the soulless dead

you gob of tobacco juice spit &
hardened above two crooked pipes

everyone hates you yes you
the wilderness that devours

the skillful thief on Farmer's Lane
sucking liquor from a ripe plum

I wanted to say I understand you
a victim of appetites so intense

you would boil yourself in broth
if only you could live to taste the flesh

Oh Nothing

just mumbling to myself
about the good old days that never were

trips to the coast where the sun did not explode
each morning in a photo of a mushroom cloud

the skiing skydiving bungee jumping never those
although we did a lot of falling spiraling down & down

autumn leaves in New England like fireworks frozen
oh to have seen them oh to have seen

we didn't dance at ritzy parties
or dress like Apaches for a costume ball

our love was simpler
holding hands in a darkened theater

arguing softly over where
we did & didn't want to eat

there was no orgy of lights in a faded wood
to mark our passage through parables of life &

oh the rocket trips to Mars
the pastel rings of Saturn like a sand mandala

yes they were so lovely so serenely circling
all those treasured times we were not there

Meeting My Lover for Lunch

the way she touches the mug to her lip
pulling the broth into her

no fury no second thoughts &
how she dabs with napkin

exterminating the superfluous
regal as a delicate tsarina

my God I have been away too long
I have walked a jagged path among the dust

I have circled I have side-stepped I have overrun
elsewhere otherwise

lost to her mouth & bird-
like scratching of her fork against the plate

bread bring us bread O Lord
I vow that I shall spare the road my hunger

Breath

I'm listening to Mozart's Flute Concerto No. 2
on my Sony Walkman & what stands out

is not the melody the speed the passion of the soloist
but her breathing—it must be a her with dark hair tied back

one lonely strand straying dangling sticking
to her damp forehead like grass to the mower's blade—

when she takes in the wind she recycles into riffs wildly
        dancing
as if from the electric guitars of Whitesnake or Van Halen

each inhale so sudden in its execution
adds its own sound to the songbird assembly line

a new fluttering for a showroom at the whistle factory
so perfectly placed like jazz notes blue as a drunken
        melancholy

it is as though the master himself in his genius his wisdom
wrote each gasp onto the clef as though a chord & also rest

yet he could not have anticipated the compact disc
headphones & proximity to sounds or orchestrations

so this is not his music but hers as she leans back
forgotten amidst the forest of the stage

her lips clawing hungrily for air &
mocking the fury of some first maddening kiss

while she gives back & she gives back
a translator adding flourishes to these forgotten words

Repentance

I always take time to read poems titled "Apology"
I crave the plot the narrative arc of the noir

in otherwise blissful sometimes centered hearts
all that anecdotal evil or at least

bad things briefly ventured like oaths
fighting words a finger extended upward

practical jokes gone beyond their parameters
who tenderly kissed his lover's sister?

who picked a pocket? filched a note?
intended tearing the heirloom velvet portrait of a horse?

I want this: all the guilt & suffering
some so freely give away

I love the violence the madness the blood-hunger &
especially the passion lust desire

all the unnatural acts men commit
to practice the wholly natural ones

so I delve again & always into these artful confessions
seeking the pin on which ugliness & beauty have their dance

hoping too that I will see you there
asking for forgiveness showing remorse

as you admit how you hid the constellations &
how you should have given me the sun

Something Important

my mother says "don't write about me
write about something important"

which could mean torn limbs of children
after a bomb attack in Syria

or nature's stormtroopers battering coasts &
attacking through faulty tectonic plates

yet more likely invites some fiction
about the mysteries of blood

that will sell a million copies
like a hardback bible of these escapes from other torments

I once told her I was reading a Michael Connelly book
about a baby-raping cop killer &

she said "good maybe you'll learn something"
which she didn't mean the way it sounded

but as a comment on the economics of popular prose
what is something important enough to write about?

just fantasy sticking its tongue in the ear of finance?
what of wars? or desires?

maybe it's the ensorcelling perfection of a sunrise
tranquility from fields of unblemished snow

she in silhouette between these things
walks outside to collect the daily paper

her breath crafts concrete poems in the air
for now I find this image is enough

The English Language

I love it because as I it is not true
neither precise nor consistent in its public face

a hodgepodge of mimicry
it lacks the illusion of permanence kept by glass

how it twists shifts undulates
splatters like a paint can smashed against a concrete wall

sometimes it stops to pick corn from its teeth
finding behind each kernel daffodils

a language of the dead who cross all borders
the jazz vocabulary & the silent prayer before a beggar's
          feast

with its constant weeping
it might seem less poetic than the French

after years of diets & cursing
it has learned a sort of comfort with itself

The Eye

disappearing from the eye is death in the opinion of the eye
which does not understand the distinction soon but merely never

a stranger stepping behind the house has fallen from a precipice
the neighbor's collie runs off following a straight line to infinity

I must at no time leave my lover by herself
she would make a ridiculous corpse

ever hateful & forgetful is the eye a brutal despoiler of reminiscence
although at least discreet in its genocide

I cannot sleep tonight I cannot sleep for fear
my eye in the long dark destroys the world

Rubbernecking

do not feel guilty though you are first to slow &
see that delicate form facedown by the stone barrier

a carpeted cadaver its lilac skin
not grayed by fall defeat & passing

no murder of crows will come to eat its guts
no overlord of highways hurries to remove its soggy meat

yet somewhere there is mourning for tenderness
those ears half-cocked as if tucked low for Mass

though no unction however extreme
will part the candied gates

now as you accelerate away from sorrow
you contemplate the land-bound dead man's float

the lack of tire tracks & torn limbs
was it suicide by open window?

was there a push into the path of an oncoming ice-
cream truck boldly ringing its funereal bells?

tonight comes silence as black as beads for eyes
strange & unforgiving calm

a lime-green bunny on the bed
leans into absence surrendering tears of dust

Letter to the Guy in the White Sedan Yelling "Hey Asshole!" at the Driver of the Burgundy Van in Front

sometimes red is a prison not easy to walk away from
after your release comes through

sometimes freedom hypnotizes like a flame
to the backward ticking *ten nine eight* of the mesmerist's voice

why hurry as you spend your life
travelling one parking lot to the next

the delay a purchased breath
when the eureka moment claps its one hand

sometimes like Siddhartha whispering the Om
stillness you learn was your destination all along

A Woman's Apartment

entering a new one that first time
penetration of the doorway's defenses

seeing the private inch by inch
like peeling away a sweater or long flowered skirt

step in & bring the tension with you
how it rubs against anticipation in your chest

each footfall is a conquering
each a plea for unshackling from business hours

why do you hesitate staring
at rows of books that define a shelf & a life

when your eyes wish to seek out ends
of dark hallways & all that stays hidden?

of course you sniff the air for traces
where a candle burned its berries & cinnamon

what now? do you sit with palms on knees?
or wait to be directed through the mysteries?

this is what you love not the lips or skin
but the strangeness after the invitation

how you would scrub dishes stacked in her sink
to steal a glimpse of floral patterns on her plates

Home Confinement

as I opened the door the deputy
said "good you're home

our computer told us you were
in the Bahamas" a spider

spilled down the mortar-gray shoulder
of his uniform—he didn't seem to notice

"I had to be sure" he told me
"although I really hoped I was going

on a trip for your extradition"
he brushed the arachnid off his arm

came in & reset the transmitter box
it happens like that: a man

thinks he's home free
when he hasn't left the house

still someone's chasing him
around corners & down blind alleys

I wanted to say "you don't see me
I'm not here" to blink & vanish

through a trap door in the stage
while he thought of sunny beaches

of women in bikinis tightly bright
like handcuffs made of flame

I thought of being invisible &
being no one as if for once

in my sordid life I wanted
the one thing that I already had

The Dictionary

I keep a dictionary by my bed
in case a word is spoken when I dream

the language of sleep plays three-card monte
with what I knew & what I have forgotten

a juggler with a dog's nose
mutters something I can't understand

an assassin demands my password &
it's there unvoiced by my second tongue

I would sacrifice speech in the hours of rest
all I want is to dance & play a green harmonica

but the notes too are little words
that need their definitions when I wake

young words played by a verbose instrument
that speaks from somewhere other than the throat

The Express

city bus lumbers to the curb
its sign flashing *Regional Jail*

the Abandon-Hope line
tourist shuttle through the lonely dark

I watch three climb aboard
no one leave—this my America

after all & who paroles
from the side streets & back roads

of America the penitentiary
America the secret detention center

suddenly I'm sweating
like a soda can in summer heat

"not me" I say "not again"
as I signal turning right where

innocence waits & I the guilty
can't get far enough away from here

In Deference to the Thunderstorm

a squirrel drinks from the fountain after rain
wet mouth browned to a hobo's five-o'clock shadow

he carries no poke on his back not
yet though his journeys will take him aboard

boxcars made from tree limbs gliding through peaceful
country afternoons away from the sickness of highways

coughing & deer trampling backward in retreat all
is stillness where gray absolves the sunlight yes

* * *

is stillness where gray absolves the sunlight? yes
I sit on a stone bench my eyes

drawn to sudden color from the torn extremities
of wildflowers cadmium bright like match head petals

burning abstractions shot across damp grass so much
violence in the wake & vibrancy so much

peace if one looks to it grayest peace
gray of headstones & the gray of rest

* * *

gray of headstones & the gray of rest
I think studying the angel on its belly

where it fell away from the rising water
triangular base a marker over such a grave

I expect a name to be written there
but only blankness as if a memorial for

83

all the earth drowned beneath grinding gears &
drowned by the storm how this laughter fades

* * *

drowned by the storm how this laughter fades
how bushes bow their battered heads & how

the smell of everything is a broken heart
I listen for songbirds hear only a police

siren miles away blaring its new wave music
that too calls attention to this stillness this

momentary after-ease I want to possess it but
cracks between fingers let the noise back in

Groom

you should should you? yes
hitchhike home one hundred miles

to your wedding
your bacchanal & stitchwork

binding skin to skin
before the kiss the feast the slow dance

into a new century stand there
on the lip of an on-ramp

signless your only luggage
a guitar case duct-taped on all sides

wear a camouflage coat
warm enough for hunting

whistle as cars go by &
sing yes sing a love song from the 70s

assume your moment like a crown
a gold ring in a wineglass

I will find you I will stop
take you in stealing your adventure

as we bisect old-wood forest
enchanted with waterfalls

that blink their jaundiced sulfur eyes
greeting us acknowledging you &

though I seem a student now
show me the miracle of the longer road

Return Visit to Morgantown, West Virginia

city of my marriage license symbol for a thing
that died a cackling chicken's death in the long grass

city of my law degree I put to good use in prison
city of my addiction to pills I carried from here

roving the spiral stiff with disappointment
look at you now spread out like an old man on his porch
      swing

a little wider at the hips & in the center
a few parts missing a few battle scars like mine &

look at me returning as your guest
broken into shards & stitched together with lines of verse

we are friends & enemies you & I
dealers of the darkness of possibility

like fortune tellers who—relegated to the fair—
cannot see the future for themselves

Letter to a Wound

grin of a toneless etching
you thumb-bound opaque lens

how you laugh in yellow light
reminding me a knife cuts all &

both sides in any war must drag
their dead from a crimson field

your presence leaves a stain
like a garden hose forgotten on the lawn

slightly brighter than the grass around
waiting to be rewound into a coil

Self-medication

early the pills pushed keys to open doors
behind which a voice huddled cringing in dim light

others brightened hues of lipstick roses crumbled in the rain
before a mower cut their muddy graves

or heightened flavors of coffee & tobacco
with sweet syrup from a lover's breath

they performed surgeries
to remove nails bullets thumbprints from the brain

I didn't realize I took so many tablets
to control my peripatetic wanderings

to sit still as I talked or wrote the nonsense that delights
the nougat in the meat of the milk chocolate

later I swallowed amber bottles plastic lids &
all to rid myself of myself

to forgive the devil gnawing my arm &
the god who stood there laughing at the wounds

oh how those capsules erased the lines blotted tastes
blurred the perfumed pages lost in some Dead Letter office

I couldn't sing without my dose of melody
dance unless a rhythm was prescribed

physician heal thyself some time was said & I
went to that doctor until his pen ran dry

Letter to Four Old Postmen Every Day at Noon Playing Dominoes at a Table in the Gino's Pizza and Spaghetti House

numbers erase the value of all else
as counting backward while an anesthetic hums its lullaby

others allow you to pound the table
fifteen twenty-five fifty you speak

as though computers touching your screens
to slide an application into place

the same in lunch & dress you stop between the bones
to gnaw at pepperoni projecting from your Italian subs

I imagine you dancing with deliveries you make
as you escape what boxes hold you like unopened letters

how you remove your winter hats &
show us you have faces

more than just pneumatic tubes
sucking our words through a straw

The Test

into a cup I pour my admission of innocence
temporal evidence in the body's court

another day passes a month a year &
suddenly half a decade devoted to the Grail

how it tests one's purity
despite the bloody errantry of past crusades

the heat strip lights up like Mars in transit
as black bars in pairs appear like a prison made from night

all because I gave myself release
expressed my nature in line art to the critic cup

it tells me not that I can do no wrong
but that wrongs I've done are done with

for at least this pause this sighing hallelujah
I walk without daggers in my eyes

without regrets without new ones anyhow
this golden mead this liquor of sobriety

After Words

I left the prison library full of poetry
I have scratched turns of phrase

in topsoil to be censored by worms
or devoured by armies of ravenous clover

the whole shebang now is a message
tagged on a boulder or side of a bridge

Jerry loves Jenna for one but more often
You don't want to know what I'm thinking

I look around & nothing seems familiar
the sonnets hide in dark places

renting space in hourly motels
or buried Paragraph 4 Subsection B

of petitions for dissolution of marriage
how they claw at strangers & beg for meat

at least the villanelles have been
rounded up & thrown in the clink

they suffer for justice there among
so many unread volumes

while out here other forms of verse
gibber all around me like a murder of crows

I stab at them & sometimes they bleed
though the louder they scream

the more they pierce their guts
with jags of cold metallic silence

Power Outage

somewhere wind or lightning licks a swooning tree
somewhere the line drags sparks like a dangling muffler

here I rest in the dreamless sleep
a panoramic depicting night minus walls windows door

the inverse of the *Eureka!* moment
stretches black for maybe hours

I can't see what I can't see & imagine what I can
as I search with dim-witted fingers

for a flashlight or sacred candle
a North Star guiding sailors in a drawer

Letter to a Droplet of Water

I watched you streak
down the tub's edge

like a star fall with clarity
along the photonegative of night

so light like a fingertip
over skin receptive to the touch

I wish I could possess you
like a firefly

in the gentle prison
of my hands

Gamble

I play the suited connectors
I play the longshots

I only bet on dogs named Ace
I bet on lethargic dogs that surprise everyone

yes I've lost money
yes bad beats

yes I'd roll snake eyes
were there no ones on the dice

were there no aces
the ivory faces blank as a glacier's

sometimes I win in spite of me
in the morgue

staring down corpses cold & mute
as *I am that I am*

one said I have honest eyes
one said I give so much away

he reads my poker face & weeps
from all the loneliness he sees

"Thanks for Ending Your Poems"

—rejection letter with typo

at first you had us hopeful all atremble
your image of the sun ablaze through early overgrowth

clearly referred to war in the Middle East
but why did you leave the light so soon

to describe graveyards of acorn husks
caskets clustered half in half out of earth?

you went on forever about the acorns
we didn't think you'd shut up about those fucking acorns

also why do squirrels keep running across your lines
like little silver missiles? —oh never mind

from there it's a tangle of indecency
hunters raising rifles in the dawn mist

deer bouncing past children in backyards
as we wait & wonder which will be shot first

brakes squeal from the highway yet we never see the crash
smell fumes or burning hair

where are the blood & skulls? where's the shock & awe?
worse there go those squirrels again frolicking on a
        fencepost

trying to squeeze a plum between their teeth
they run on & on through all of history

until let's face it you have nothing left to say &
like an obnoxious wedding guest say more

About the Author

Ace Boggess is a freelance writer and editor living in Charleston, West Virginia. His books include two previous poetry collections, *The Prisoners* and *The Beautiful Girl Whose Wish Was Not Fulfilled*, and the novel *A Song Without a Melody*. He earned degrees from Marshall University (B.A.) and the West Virginia University College of Law (J.D.). He received a fellowship from the West Virginia Commission on the Arts. His writing has appeared in *Harvard Review*, *Notre Dame Review*, *North Dakota Quarterly*, *RATTLE*, *The Chattahoochee Review*, and many other journals.

BRICK ROAD

POETRY PRESS

Our Mission

The mission of Brick Road Poetry Press is to publish and promote poetry that entertains, amuses, edifies, and surprises a wide audience of appreciative readers. We are not qualified to judge who deserves to be published, so we concentrate on publishing what we enjoy. Our preference is for poetry geared toward dramatizing the human experience in language rich with sensory image and metaphor, recognizing that poetry can be, at one and the same time, both familiar as the perspiration of daily labor and as outrageous as a carnival sideshow.

BRICKROAD

POETRY PRESS

Also Available from Brick Road Poetry Press

www.brickroadpoetrypress.com

Dancing on the Rim by Clela Reed
Possible Crocodiles by Barry Marks
Pain Diary by Joseph D. Reich
Otherness by M. Ayodele Heath
Drunken Robins by David Oates
Damnatio Memoriae by Michael Meyerhofer
Lotus Buffet by Rupert Fike
The Melancholy MBA by Richard Donnelly
Two-Star General by Grey Held
Chosen by Toni Thomas
Etch and Blur by Jamie Thomas
Water-Rites by Ann E. Michael

BRICKROAD

POETRY PRESS

About the Prize

The Brick Road Poetry Prize, established in 2010, is awarded annually for the best book-length poetry manuscript. Entries are accepted August 1st through November 1st. The winner receives $1000 and publication. For details on our preferences and the complete submission guidelines, please visit our website at www.brickroadpoetrypress.com.

www.ingramcontent.com/pod-product-compliance
Lightning Source LLC
Chambersburg PA
CBHW022013090426
42741CB00007B/1021